KT-461-005

WITHDRAWN
~~SERVICE~~

2100066840

E.L.R.S.

FOOD WE ATE

STEWART ROSS

641. (i)

S 328292

Stewart Ross

STARTING HISTORY

Food We Ate
How We Travelled
Our Families
Our Holidays
Our Schools
Shopping
What We Wore
Where We Lived

Series Editor: Kathryn Smith
Series Designer: Derek Lee

First published in 1991 by
Wayland (Publishers) Ltd
61 Western Road, Hove
East Sussex, BN3 1JD

© Copyright 1991 Wayland (Publishers) Ltd

British Library Cataloguing in Publication Data
  Ross, Stewart
  Food We Ate
  1. Great Britain. Social life, history
  I. Title II. Series
  941

ISBN 0 7502 0144 4

Typeset by Dorchester Typesetting Group Ltd
Printed and bound in Belgium by Casterman S.A.

Acknowledgements

Birdseye Walls 11; Eye Ubiquitous 4, 17, 19 (top), 27 (top) Chris Fairclough 16, 24, 28; Mary Evans 7 (bottom); J. Heinrich 7 (top), 13 (top), 23 (top), 29 (top); Hulton *cover*, 5, 9, 12, 13 (bottom), 15, 21, 23 (bottom), 26, 27, 29; Imperial War Museum 22; Topham 6, 19, 25; Wayland Picture Library 8, 20; T. Woodcock 4; Zefa 10, 14, 18.

Words that appear in **bold** are explained in the glossary on page 31.

Starting History is designed to be used as source material for Key Stage One of the National History Curriculum. The main text and photographs reflect the requirements of AT1 (Understanding history in its setting) and AT3 (Acquiring and evaluating historical information). The personal accounts are intended to introduce different points of view (AT2 – Understanding points of view and interpretations) and suggestions for activities and further research (AT3 – Development of ability to acquire evidence from historical sources) can be found on page 30.

CONTENTS

This family is having breakfast. Can you remember what you had for breakfast today? Perhaps you had **cereal** and toast, or an egg. Which cereal do you like best?

Have you noticed how many different kinds of food there are to choose from? People have not always had such a choice. The food we eat has changed a lot over the last seventy-five years.

This family is having Sunday lunch. The picture was taken in 1954. Were your mum and dad alive then? How can you tell that this is an old picture?

In those days many families ate large meals together. Often the food took a long time to **prepare**. Not many dads helped in the kitchen.

This picture is even older than the last one. It shows a fish **stall** in 1932. Do you know anyone who was alive then?

At that time most food was not sold in packets. There was not much frozen food either. Cooks had to do much of the work themselves, using fresh **produce**.

Mabel Rowe is now eighty-seven years old. Her parents were rich. She can remember the parties they had for their friends.

'The picture reminds me of my parents' dinner parties. It's hard to believe now. They all sat in the dining-room, where servants brought them mountains of food. But I was too young to join in. I went in to say goodnight to everyone before I went to bed. When I chatted to the servants, my father scolded me for bad manners.'

SCHOOL DINNERS

It is dinner time at school. The children in the picture have brought sandwiches. Do you eat sandwiches or school dinners?

Ask your parents what they ate at school. Were their meals the same as yours? Today we understand more about a healthy **diet**. Canned drinks and crisps taste nice, but they are not very good for us.

Look at the little girl on the left of this picture. Do you think she likes her school dinner?

The photograph was taken just after the **Second World War**. At that time all children had free school dinners. Children were also given free milk. This was to make sure that everyone got enough **vitamins**. Do your parents remember free school milk?

This family is shopping in the **supermarket**. All the things in their trolley are wrapped up, in packets or in bottles. The packaging protects the food.

Today we buy most of our food in tins and packets. Sometimes it is frozen. Which foods do we buy fresh, without any wrapping?

This is an **advertisement** from 1955 for fish fingers. Fish fingers were a new idea then. Most people bought fresh fish from a **fishmonger** and prepared it at home.

Frozen food can be kept for a long time in a fridge. But fifty years ago many families did not have a fridge. They had to go shopping almost every day.

Here is a food cupboard in 1939. Were your grandparents alive then?

Look at what is in the cupboard. Which things can we still buy today? If you look carefully at the cocoa tin, you can see how much it cost. Ask a grown-up how much 2d is in modern money.

Before the Second World War most sweets were kept in large jars. There were no sweet wrappers. Graham Black went into a sweet shop with his pocket money every week.

'We loved Mrs Moore's shop. The smell made my mouth water. We chose our sweets, then she weighed them on her **scales**. If she was in a good mood, she gave us one free. One Christmas she gave me a whole penny bar of chocolate. It was huge.'

HAVE A DRINK

How many different drinks can you think of? Fifty years ago, there were not nearly so many.

Putting fizzy drinks in cans or plastic bottles is a new idea. Drinks used to be sold in glass bottles. Today, we can collect empty bottles and cans and **recycle** them.

This photograph was taken over forty years ago. The men are enjoying a tea break. Tea has always been a very popular drink in this country.

When your grandparents were children there were no tea bags or instant coffee powder. Tea was sold loose in packets. Coffee was **ground** from coffee beans. Today there are many more drinks to choose from.

Do you know what fast food is? These children are having a meal in a fast food **restaurant**. Their burgers and chips were ready to eat as soon as they went in.

You can eat fast food in the restaurant or take it out to eat somewhere else. When your mum and dad were children there were very few fast food restaurants.

Do you have porridge for breakfast? It used to take all night to prepare. Now we can make it in just a few minutes, using special quick oats.

This woman is eating porridge that took only a few minutes to cook. In the last fifty years preparing food has become much quicker and easier. Do you know why?

This man is baking . Before the Second
World War many families made their
own bread. They often made their own
cakes and biscuits too.

Have you ever made bread at home?
Baking takes a long time, but it fills the
house with a lovely smell.

When Harry Baker was young the only take-away food was fish and chips. A fish and chip van visited his street every Friday.

'When the van arrived you could smell the fried food right down the street. The man in the van was called Alf. His face was fat and shiny. He wrapped our fish and chips in newspaper to keep them warm. The whole meal cost one shilling – that's 5p. I loved fish and chips on a Friday night, but I don't think all that grease was very good for us.'

19

Can you see any machines in this kitchen?
There is a mixer, a microwave oven and a
modern fridge. These machines help to
prepare meals quickly and easily.

Forty years ago there were not as many
helpful machines. Ask your grandparents
what kitchens were like when they
were young.

This woman is hard at work preparing dinner. There are no time-saving machines in her kitchen. She is cooking on a gas stove. How is it different from the cooker in your home?

The picture was taken in 1939. At that time most married women did not go out to work. They stayed at home to do the housework and cooking. It could take them hours to prepare a meal.

What is the message of this poster? It came out during the Second World War. There was a shortage of food then.

Families could only buy a certain amount of food each week. For example, each person was allowed four teaspoons of sugar a day. This was called rationing. Not many people got fat during the war.

SAVE BREAD
and you save lives
SERVE
POTATOES
& you serve the country

Jenny Williams belonged to Wimbledon tennis club during the war. She is wearing her white tennis dress in the picture below.

'We were always short of meat in wartime. Farms were set up in all sorts of odd places. One day I saw these men bringing pigs into the tennis club. They had built a pigsty near the courts. It smelt terrible. I didn't play much after that.'

Where do you think this photograph was taken? In China? No! It was taken a short time ago in this country.

Nowadays the food we eat is more exciting than it was forty years ago. We have a much wider choice. In many towns you can find food from all over the world.

This family is on holiday in France. They are enjoying French food. Most people did not travel **abroad** for their holidays until about 1960.

These days millions of British people go abroad every year. They bring back new ideas about things to eat and drink. Do you know where these foods come from: spaghetti; croissants; curry?

These American soldiers came to Britain during the Second World War. Ask your grandparents if they remember meeting any American soldiers.

The Americans brought some of their own food with them. Since then American food, such as burgers, has become very popular here. The Americans call chips french fries. Sometimes we use that name too.

Will Carlton was eight when the picture below was taken in 1949. He remembers what his family meals were like then.

'I was the boy with big ears in the front of this picture. We were having Sunday lunch. Every week we had the same thing — meat and two vegetables. We had never heard of pizza or burgers.

We were very fussy. If we had been given spaghetti for dinner, instead of spuds, we would have thrown our plates on the floor.'

IS IT GOOD FOR YOU?

Do you read the labels on food packets? They tell you exactly what is inside.

These days many food packets have tiny amounts of special **ingredients**. They make the food look good, last longer or taste better. These ingredients are not always healthy. Doctors say we should eat more fresh foods, like people used to.

Liz Cooke's mother had fifteen children. It was not easy to feed them all. The family bought lots of bread, butter, sugar and sausages.

'Here we are unloading the shopping for the weekend. Look at all that sliced white bread! We thought it was very good for us.

Today people eat more brown bread, with bits in it – just like my granny made. We are going back to the old days. Funny, isn't it?'

29

Talking to people

Ask grown-ups you know well about what they ate when they were young. They can tell you how food has changed since they were children. Farmers know a lot about the sort of food people like to buy. If you know a farmer, ask him or her about the changes they have seen.

Using your eyes

Look in old books, papers and magazines to find out about food in the past. See if you can find an old cookery book and compare it with a modern one. Ask a grown-up if they will help you make one of the old recipes. Old advertisements will also tell you about food that used to be popular.

Making shopping lists

You could make a shopping list of food we eat today. Write down how much things cost, and draw pictures of them. Then make a list for twenty years ago, forty years ago and so on. See how far back you can go. Your teacher might like to make a display of your lists on the wall.

Read all about it

The pictures in these books will help you to find out more about the food people ate in the past:

At Home in the 1950s, Shirley Echlin (Longman, 1988)

Children in the Second World War, Elizabeth Merson
   (Longman, 1983)

At Home in the 1930s, Sallie Purkis (Longman, 1983)

Looking at Food, Nina Sully (Batsford, 1984)

GLOSSARY

Abroad Out of this country.

Advertisement A message asking you to buy something. You see advertisements on TV and in magazines.

Cereal Breakfast food which comes in packets, like cornflakes.

Diet All the food we eat.

Fishmonger Someone who sells fish.

Formal Smart and tidy.

Ground Crushed to powder.

Ingredients What something is made of. The label on a food packet tells you all its ingredients.

Prepare Make ready.

Produce Food grown on a farm.

Recycle To use something again.

Restaurant An eating house where people buy meals.

Scales Machines for telling how heavy something is. Food shops have scales on the counter.

Second World War The war which lasted from 1939 to 1945. The fighting spread all round the world.

Stall A large table on which things are sold in the open air. You see stalls at markets.

Supermarket A huge shop which sells all kinds of food.

Vitamins Vitamins are found in foods such as vegetables, fruit and milk. We need them for good health and to grow.

INDEX